Sound Advice on

RECORDING & MIXING DRUMS

by Bill Gibson

447 Georgia Street
Vallejo, CA 94590
(707) 554-1935

Publisher: Mike Lawson
Art Director: Stephen Ramirez; Editor: Patrick Runkle
Editorial Assistant: Heather Johnson
PortaStudio 2488 cover image courtesy of Tascam

ProAudio Press is an imprint of artistpro.com, LLC
447 Georgia Street
Vallejo, CA 94590
(707) 554-1935

Also from the ProMusic Press InstantPro Series
Sound Advice on Microphone Techniques
Sound Advice on Compressors, Limiters, Expanders & Gates
Sound Advice on Developing Your Home Studio
Sound Advice on MIDI Production
Sound Advice on Equalizers, Reverbs & Delays
Sound Advice on Mixing

Also from EMBooks
Making the Ultimate Demo, 2nd Ed.
Making Music with Your Computer, 2nd Ed.
Anatomy of a Home Studio

Also from MixBooks
The AudioPro Home Recording Course, Volumes I, II, and III
The Art of Mixing: A Visual Guide to Recording, Engineering, and Production
The Mixing Engineer's Handbook
The Mastering Engineer's Handbook
Music Publishing: The Real Road to Music Business Success, Rev. and Exp. 5th Ed.
Critical Listening and Auditory Perception
Professional Microphone Techniques
Sound for Picture, 2nd Ed.
Music Producers, 2nd Ed.
Live Sound Reinforcement
Professional Sound Reinforcement Techniques
Creative Music Production: Joe Meek's Bold Techniques

Printed in Auburn Hills, MI
ISBN 1-931140-37-5

Contents

The Percussion Family 5

Drum Conditioning 6

Theories of Drum Miking 17

Recording Level 21

Acoustic Considerations 23

Equalizing Drums 39

Kick Drum 42

Snare Drum 48

Toms 49

Overhead Microphones 51

The Hi-hat Mic 54

Gating the Drum Tracks 57

Application of Techniques 59

Effects On Drums 66

Compressing Drums 67

Panning the Drums 71

Compare Your Work 73

Triggering During Mixdown 76

Automation 78

Conclusion 79

The Percussion Family

Most people haven't listened enough with analytical ears to decide what they like and dislike about certain drum sounds. They have nothing on which to base their opinions. When considering drum sounds, there are some common characteristics that exist in drum sounds that most of us would call good. The term good is obviously subject to individual opinion. A good drum sound must also be appropriate for the musical style of the song that it's in. Good drum sounds will almost always have:

- Clean highs that blend with the mix
- Solid lows that blend with the mix
- Enough mids to feel punch
- Not so many mids that the sound is muddy
- Natural sound that possesses a warm tone
- Dimension, often sounding larger than life

- Believably appropriate reverberation
- Balance and blend in the mix

The most important thing you can do at this point is listen to a lot of different styles of music that have been recorded in a lot of different studios by a lot of different top-notch professionals. Subject yourself to a large quantity of music. Try to be very analytical about the sounds you're hearing. It's one thing to let the music passively cross your ears, it's another to actually hear what's going on texturally, musically and sonically.

Drum Conditioning

To get good drums sounds, it's necessary to be familiar with drum tuning and dampening techniques. A bad sounding drum is nearly impossible to get a good recorded sound from. A good sounding drum can make your recording experience much more enjoyable.

If the drum heads are dented and stretched out, cancel the rest of your appointments for the day. You'll be spending a substantial amount of time getting an acceptable drum sound.

If the drums aren't high quality instruments, there's a good chance that the shells aren't smooth and level, and there's a possibility that the drums aren't even perfectly round. If this is the case, the heads won't seat evenly on the drum shell and there'll be a loss of tone, detracting from the drum sound.

Tuning

Often, the difference between a good sounding drum and a bad sounding drum lies simply in tuning. The standard approach to tuning involves:

- Tuning the top head to the tone that you want

- Making sure the pitch is the same all the way around the head by tapping at each lug and adjusting the lugs until they all match
- Duplicating the sound of the top head with the bottom head

If the head isn't tuned evenly all the way around, the head won't resonate well. You'll probably hear more extraneous overtones than smooth tone.

Audio Example 1

A Poorly Tuned Tom

Drum Sticks

The drummer's choice of sticks and their condition can make a big difference in the sound of the drums. Nylon-tipped sticks have a brighter sounding attack than wood-tipped sticks, especially on cymbals. Hickory sticks have a different sound than oak sticks, and they both sound different than graphite or metal sticks. Heavy sticks have a completely different sound than light sticks.

Most experienced studio drummers carry several different types of drum sticks with them, even though they probably have their own overall favorite.

If you want to be prepared when recording drums, it's worth the investment to have some extra sticks available that vary in size and physical composition.

Muffling Drums

There are several techniques for muffling and dampening drum tone. Trends shift with time and genre. Whereas drums of one era and style are highly controlled and dampened, drums of the next are open and free. It's your job to stay in touch with current trends, adjusting your techniques accordingly.

Don't use muffling as a substitute for a well-tuned drum. It's hard to beat the sound of a great drum with great natural tone. I try to use dampening technique to lightly control unwanted overtones which I know will be difficult to deal with during mixdown.

Try each of the illustrated dampening techniques to hear the difference in the sound of each approach. I've gotten great sounds by using self-adhering weather stripping and a product called Moon Gel, applying the amount of material in the positions that create the sound I want. Moon Gel is a jello-like solid rectangle, approximately 1 by 1.5 by .125 inches. This is a very flexible approach. Both Moon Gel and the foam weather stripping are easy to move around for the desired sound and they provide an even, natural-sound and appealing dampening. Moon Gel sticks to the head much like weather stripping without the sticky residue.

Dampening with Duct Tape

Stick a piece of duct tape to the top and/or bottom head to control ringing. Add as much as needed to get the desired sound. Placing tape near the rim usually works best.

This technique works equally well on the kick, snare or toms.

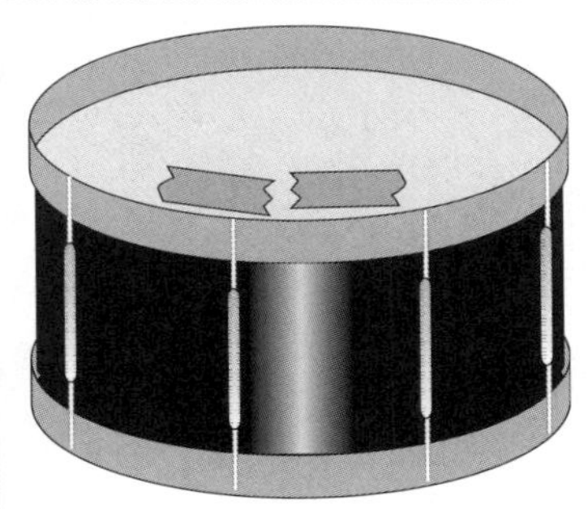

Dampening With Facial Tissue

Use duct tape or masking tape to hold facial tissue, cotton or gauze on the head. Add as much as needed to get the desired sound. Placing tape near the rim usually works best.

This technique works equally well on the kick, snare or toms.

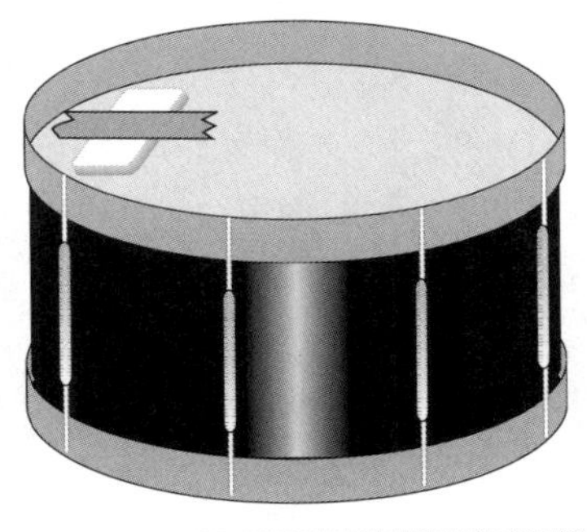

Dampening With a Wallet

1. Lay a billfold on top of the drum near the rim. Bring duct tape up over the rim and onto the wallet.

2. It's not necessary for the tape to touch the head. The wallet can move freely for a natural sound and feel.

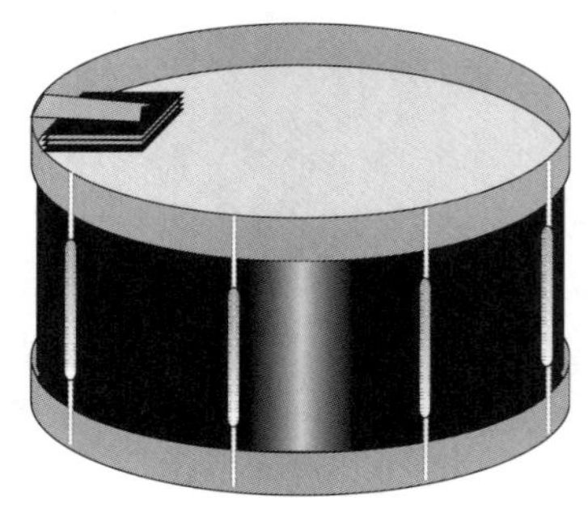

A Cloth Strip Under the Head

1. A 1–3 inch wide strip of cloth (like a piece of an old sheet) can be sandwiched between the head and the shell about 2–6 inches from the side of the drum.

2. As you tighten the head, pull the cloth taut with the excess still hanging out from under the head.

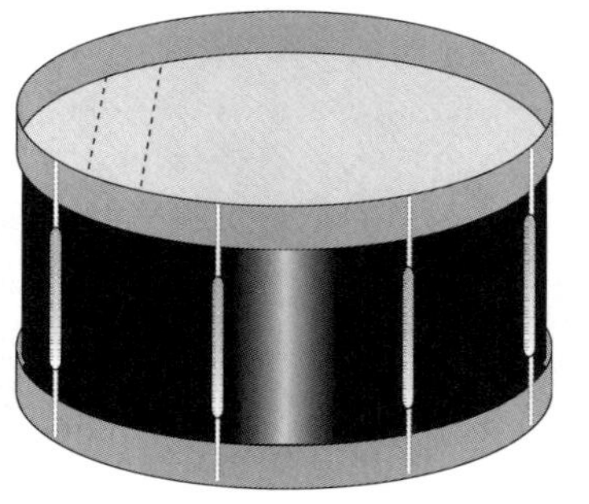

Dampening With a Head Ring

1. Cut a 1–2 inch wide ring from the outer part of an old drum head—these are also commercially available.

2. Lay the ring on top of your drum head to evenly dampen the tone. The closer the ring is to the rim, the smaller the amount of dampening. Keep in place with small pieces of duct tape if necessary.

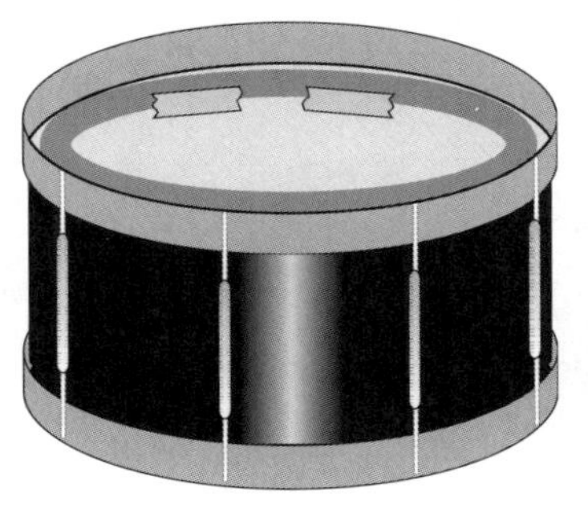

The Internal Muffler

1. A felt pad is moved up against the head from inside the drum.

2. A knob on the outside of the drum controls the positioning of the pad inside. Turn clockwise to move the pad against the head and counterclockwise to move it away.

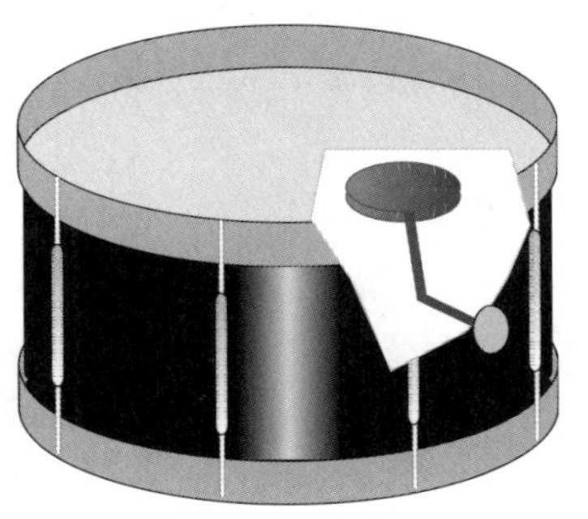

Dampening the Kick Drum

1. Set a pillow or blanket inside the kick with the front head off the drum. A duck down pillow is most adjustable and results in a full, punchy sound with good tone. For more tone put the front head back on. A 6—10 inch hole provides access for a mic with minimal effect on tone.

2. Use something like a brick or mic stand base to keep the pillow or blanket in place.

3. The pillow or blanket should touch the head. The more it touches the head the greater the dampening.

4. Check with your local music store for the hottest new dampening system.

Weather Stripping or Moon Gel

1. Use 3–6 inch pieces of self-adhering weather stripping or a piece of Moon Gel to dampen the head. Use multiple strips to fine-tune the sound of the drum if necessary. 2. Placing the weather stripping near the rim usually produces the warmest and purest tone.

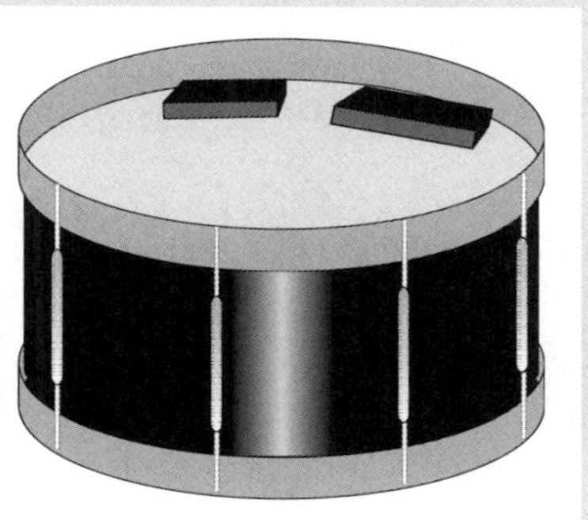

Hardware

Hardware matters. It provides a stable and solid foundation for drum tone. The drum hardware is a good indicator of overall product quality and attention to detail. Drums with excellent hardware will almost always sound better than drums with sub-standard hardware.

Shells that are true and hoops that are meticulously crafted make your job a lot easier. If the head does not make even contact around the shell it's very difficult to get good tone from the drum.

Mounting hardware design is also crucial, especially tom mounts. Any mount system that lets the drum float, with no screwed-in hardware, provides the drum the opportunity to sing. Imagine screwing a large bracket to the face of an acoustic guitar—it's easy to imagine there might be a change in the sound. The same is true for drums. A company called RIMS makes a great mount system that holds the drum by a set of lugs—the difference in sound is notable. Most major drum manufacturers currently have a free-floating tom mount system.

I've never had good luck miking floor toms with legs. The tone seems to transfer through the legs to the floor. Whenever possible, mount floor toms on a stand and suspend them from free-floating mount like the RIMS system.

Whenever possible avoid mounting anything on the kick drum. Toms and cymbals should be mounted on separate stands, not on brackets screwed into the kick drum. The more freedom any drum has from contact with any other solid object, the better it will sound.

Theories of Drum Miking

Most of the drum sounds you hear on albums are achieved through the use of several microphones recorded separately to several tracks that are blended and balanced during the mixdown. This is ideal. Practically speaking, most people don't have a pile of microphones to use at home, let alone 8 to 12 available tracks on the multitrack for drums. Most people have one or two microphones, and these microphones weren't purchased with drums or percussion in mind, but as your setup and skills build you'll want to build your arsenal of task-specific microphones.

Essential Microphones

You should have a good condenser mic for over the drum set and for cymbals. Condensers are the mic of choice for percussion, and they do the best job of capturing the true sound of each instrument. The fact that condenser microphones respond to transients more accurately than the other types of microphones makes them an obvious choice for percussion instruments, like tambourine, shaker, cymbals, triangle, claves or guiro.

Mic Choices

The mic of choice for close-miking toms, snare and kick is a moving-coil mic, like a Shure SM57, Sennheiser 421 or Electro-Voice RE20. Though they don't have the transient response of condenser microphones, moving-coil microphones work great for close-miking drums because they can withstand intense amounts of volume before distorting. Also, most moving-coil microphones have a built-in sensitivity in the upper frequency range, which provides an EQ that accentuates the attack of the drum.

Finding the Drum Tone

1. To hear the tone of the drum (the head ringing), place the mic near the rim.
2. To hear the attack of the drum place the mic near the center of the head.
3. Move the mic from the rim to the center of the drum until you hear the sound you like, but be sure to keep it out of the drummer's way.
4. When you're sampling a single hit, find the perfect spot for the mic, then be careful not to hit the mic.
5. Be aware that the point of contact where the stick hits the head also affects the sound of the drum. When the stick hits near the center, the sound has more attack. When the stick hits near the rim, the sound has more tone.

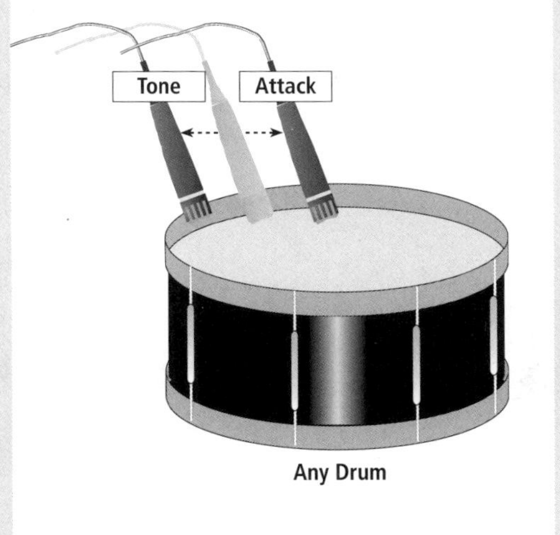

Most reasonably priced condenser and moving-coil microphones can give you good results. Don't overlook the obscure. As trends come and go we all start to hunt for unique and interesting sounds that imprint a sonic personality. Keep all the mics you can get your hands on. Even a cheap lo-fi mic might be the perfect tool to create an interesting and musical sound.

Positioning the Microphones

Keep the mic out of the drummer's way because a stick hitting the mic can ruin a take or even a microphone. Most mic manufacturers make microphones that are designed for getting into tight spots like drum sets. If the mic has to be pointing straight across the drum due to space restriction, there will be more cross-leakage between drums. It's best to point the mics at the drums, 1–2 inches away, and at an angle of 30–45 degrees.

It's best to use a mic stand for each drum mic, rather than using stands that mount on the drum rims. The less that touches the drum, the better the tone.

Recording Level

Digital

If you're using a digital recorder, don't push the drum levels above the meter's peak. The digital recording process has a pretty hard ceiling. There is no benefit to exceeding the preset maximum digital recording level. A couple of the mastering engineers I work with push digital levels beyond their intended maximum in an effort to create compact discs that are the loudest on the block. Their equipment is meticulously maintained and they have plenty of headroom in their systems, which are designed to push the limits. They win most of the awards for doing it the best, but when engineering a digital recording, we don't need to exceed maximum digital recording levels.

Analog

Sometimes it's very desirable to record drums tracks (except the overheads and hi-hat) at analog levels exceeding 0VU. A drum that's been recorded hot (in the range of +2 to +5VU) won't usually give a buzzing kind of distortion; as the analog tape reaches the point where it can't handle more magnetism, it will usually give the drum a compressed rather than distorted sound. This point is called the point of oversaturation. The sound of analog tape approaching the point of oversaturation has become an effect in its own right for recording drums. It's common for kick and toms to be recorded very hot to analog tape specifically for the sound this technique produces. It's also common for kick, snare and toms to be recorded at 0VU (or colder) to ensure that the transient will be accurately recorded. These are musically based decisions that you can make if you're stylistically aware or creatively attuned.

Acoustic Considerations

Music is about creativity and passion. It is as valid to capture drums with one mic as with twenty. The pertinence is determined by musical and artistic evaluation, not the track count.

Mic placement is the main concern when using one mic to record the drums. Where you place the mic in relation to the drums is the primary determining factor of balance between the drums and intimacy of the drum sounds.

Including the acoustic sound of the room that the drums are in makes a big difference in the sound of the track. The amount of room sound that you include in the drum track can totally change the effect of the drum part. The sound of the room that the drum set is in plays a very important role in the sound of the drum track, especially if you use a distant miking technique.

With the advent of high-quality portable recording systems based on a laptop computer and a small audio interface you're no longer limited to recording the drums in one substandard acoustical space. Try moving the recorder and the drums into a warehouse, concert hall or gymnasium. Recording in these larger spaces can give your drum sounds punch, life and character that simply can't be electronically duplicated.

Recording a Drum Set With One Microphone

Listen to the examples of a complete drum set recorded with one microphone. Audio Examples 2–5 all use the same drum set in the same studio.

Mic in Front

In this Audio Example the drum set was recorded with one mic directly in front of the kit, pointed at the set and about six feet from the floor.

One Mic in Front

This setup uses a condenser microphone with a cardioid pickup pattern positioned in front of the set, pointed at the set, approximately 6 feet above the floor.

Audio Example 3

Mic Over the Drummer's Head

In Audio Example 3 the mic is behind the kit, just above the drummer's head and pointed at the kit.

One Mic Over the Drummer's Head

This setup uses a condenser microphone with a cardioid pickup pattern behind the kit, directly over the drummer's head, pointed at the set, about 6 feet above the floor.

Overhead

In Audio Example 4 the mic is about four feet above the set and is pointed down at the drums. When a mic is placed over the drums and points down at the set, it's called an overhead.

One Mic Overhead

This setup uses one cardioid condenser microphone pointed down at the drums from a distance of about 4 feet.

Audio Example 5

Eight Feet Away

Finally, in Audio Example 5 we hear the drum set from one mic, positioned about eight feet away and pointed toward the kit.

One Mic Eight Feet Away

Most mics that look like this hear sound from the side, not the top. This setup uses a condenser mic with a cardioid or omnidirectional pickup pattern 8 feet from the kit, pointed toward the drums.

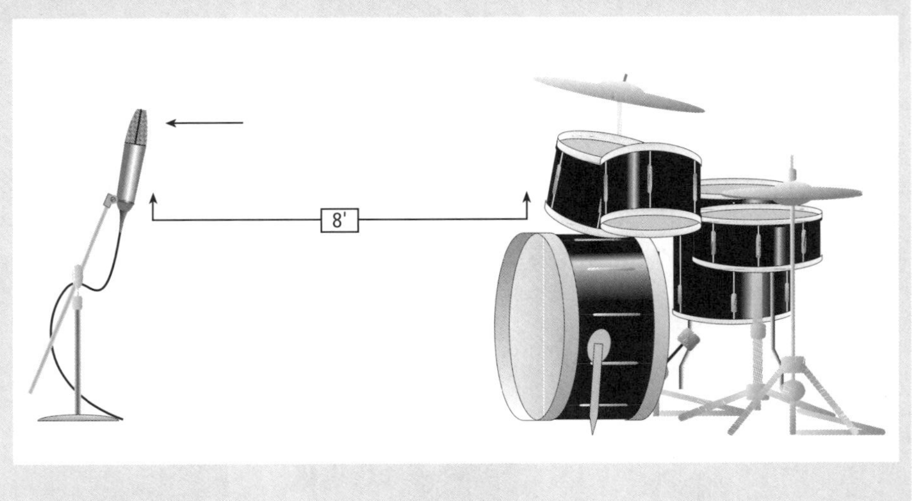

Recording a Kit with Two Mics

With two microphones on the set there are two primary options: you can use both mics together in a stereo configuration or you can use one mic for overall pickup while using the other for a specific instrument.

In Audio Example 6, I've set one mic directly over the kit with the second mic in the kick drum. When you use one of the microphones for the overall kit sound you can place the second mic on the kick drum (or possibly the snare) to get individual control, punch and definition in the mix. Choosing to close-mike the kick or the snare is purely a musical decision that's dependent on the drum part and the desired effect in the arrangement. This mic setup is more flexible than the single mic technique, but we're still limited to a monaural sound since the kick or snare would almost always be positioned in the center of the mix with the rest of the set.

Audio Example 6

One Mic Over Kit, One in the Kick

One Mic Overhead, One In the Kick

1. One cardioid condenser microphone is pointing down at the kit.

2. One cardioid moving-coil microphone is inside the kick drum, aimed at the head, about halfway between the center of the head and the shell.

Audio Example 7 uses the two condenser microphones with cardioid polar patterns as a stereo pair. The two mics are placed in a traditional X-Y configuration, directly above the drum set, at a distance of approximately three feet above the cymbals, pointing down at the drums. With this configuration, we can get a sound that has a stereo spread. As we get into the mixing process, we'll see that positioning supportive instruments away from the center of the mix helps us hear the solo parts that are typically positioned in the center of the mix.

Audio Example 7

Stereo X-Y

Stereo X-Y

Two condenser microphones are 3 feet above the cymbals. The mikes are at a 90 degree angle to each other, pointing down at the drums. With this X-Y configuration, the mic capsules should be positioned on the same horizontal and vertical plane. They should be close enough to each other so that they're nearly touching.

Try the X-Y configuration from different distances and in different rooms. Stereo mic technique is often the best choice for a very natural drum sound, but for contemporary commercial drum sounds, it lacks flexibility.

Another good two-mic technique involves placing one mic on each side of the drummer's head, level with their ears pointing forward toward the drums. Position the microphones with their capsules three to six inches from the drummer's ears to achieve a good stereo image. The drummer's skull will act as a baffle between the two microphones. Audio Example 8 demonstrates this technique.

Audio Example 8

Head Baffle

Head Baffle

Two cardioid condenser microphones are positioned level with the drummer's ears, pointing toward the front of the kit. The mics are 4–8 inches from the drummer's head.

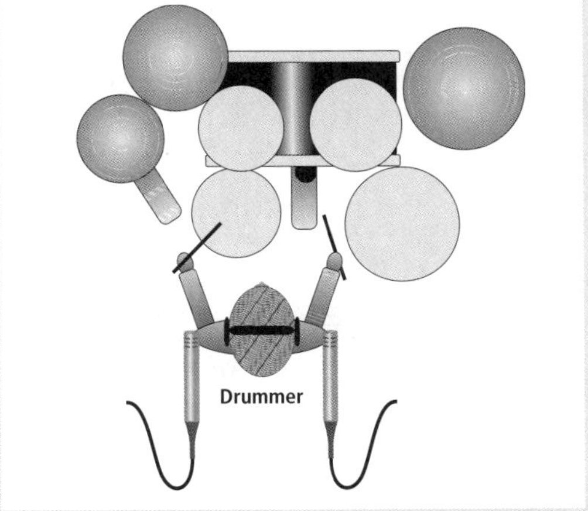

Recording a Kit with Three Mics

If you use one mic on the kick, one mic on the snare and one overhead mic, separate control of the kick and snare is possible. With three microphones, this technique will yield the most commercial and punchy sound. The kick and snare are the two main contributors to the definition of style. Being able to fine-tune their level, EQ and effects is an advantage. The drum set in Audio Example 9 was miked with one mic inside the kick, one mic two inches above the snare and one mic about two feet above the cymbals. This configuration produces the most commercially viable results so far, but it doesn't provide a stereo image of the set. The kick, snare and overhead are almost always positioned together in the center.

Audio Example 9

Three Microphones

Three Microphones

1. One cardioid condenser mic placed 2 feet above the cymbals, pointing down at the set.

2. One cardioid moving-coil mic pointing at the snare, from a distance of approximately 2 inches.

3. One cardioid moving-coil mic inside the kick, positioned for the best sound.

If we use a kick and two overheads, we can get a stereo image of the kit, but we lose individual control of the snare. Another option is to put the single mic on the snare instead of the kick, combining that mic with the two overheads. This can be a usable option, but we sacrifice control of the kick. Audio Example 10 demonstrates the sound of a drum set with two microphones overhead, in an X-Y configuration, combined with one mic inside the kick.

Audio Example 10

X-Y Overhead, One in the Kick

X-Y and Kick

1. Two cardioid condenser microphones in a traditional X-Y configuration above the kit. Experiment with placement and distance above the kit to find the appropriate musical sound.

2. One cardioid moving-coil mic inside the kick.

Recording a Kit with Four Mics

With four microphones on the set, you begin to have good control over the kick and snare sounds, plus you can get a stereo image. Some very acceptable drum sounds can be achieved using a setup with one kick mic, one snare mic, and two overheads. You'll need to experiment with placement of the microphones (especially the overheads), but solid and unique kick and snare drum sounds are possible with this mic technique. The individual microphones plus the overheads used in a stereo configuration can provide an excellent stereo image. The set in Audio Example 11 was miked with one kick mic, one snare mic and two overheads in an X-Y configuration.

Audio Example 11

Snare, Kick and X-Y

Kick, Snare, and X-Y

1. Two cardioid condenser microphones in a traditional X-Y configuration above the kit. Experiment with placement and distance above the kit to find the appropriate musical sound.

2. One cardioid moving-coil mic inside the kick.

3. One cardioid moving-coil mic pointed at the top of the snare drum, from a distance of about 2 inches above the top head.

Close-mike Technique

The most common approach to getting good, punchy, drum sounds that have unique character is to use the close-mic technique. Each drum will typically have its own mic. Each of these microphones plus two overheads will be printed to separate tracks of the multitrack. These tracks will either stay separate until the mix-down, or they might be combined with the assignment buses and bounced to stereo tracks, making room for more instruments or voices.

The drum set in Audio Example 12 is set up with one kick mic, one snare mic, one mic on each tom, two microphones overhead in an X-Y pattern and one hi-hat mic.

Audio Example 12

Snare, Kick, Toms and X-Y

Kick, Snare, Toms, X-Y Close Miking

1. Two cardioid condenser microphones in a traditional X-Y configuration above the kit. Experiment with placement and distance above the kit to find the appropriate musical sound.
2. One cardioid moving-coil mic inside the kick.
3. One cardioid moving-coil mic pointed at the top of the snare drum from a distance of about 2 inches above the top head.
4. One cardioid moving-coil mic pointed at the floor tom.
5. One cardioid moving-coil mic aimed between the upper two toms and positioned so that the two drums are balanced and blended.

Equalizing Drums

These equalization guidelines apply to the recording of basic tracks as well as mix-down. It's best to be conservative in the application of EQ on the actual recorded track. Save the extremes and "fancy" stuff for mixdown. Radical EQ and sound shaping is difficult to undo, after the fact. However, a good solid tone can be molded and formed into whatever is musically appropriate during mixdown.

Always find the microphone, mic placement and tuning that sound the best on any drum before beginning the equalization process.

The nature of close-miking a kick drum typically produces a raw sound that's overly abundant in lower midrange frequencies between 200 and 600 Hz, and the sound usually needs EQ to be usable.

When I listen to a raw close-miked drum sound before it's been equalized, I first listen for the frequencies that are clouding the sound of the kick. That frequency range is almost always somewhere between 200 and 600 Hz. Listen to the kick in Audio

Example 13 as I turn down a one-octave wide bandwidth centered at 300 Hz.

Audio Example 13

Cut 300 Hz

Once the lower mid frequencies are turned down, I'll usually address the low frequencies between 75 and 150 Hz. On the kick drum and maybe the low toms I might boost a frequency bandwidth in this range. On toms, snare, hi-hat and overheads I'll typically cut the frequencies below 100–200 Hz. This opens up the sound of the set and lets you isolate the sound of these higher drums.

Next, I'll typically locate an upper frequency to boost that'll emphasize the attack of the beater or stick hitting the instrument. Boosting a frequency between 3 and 5 kHz will usually emphasize this attack. Listen to the kick in Audio Example 14. A moving-coil mic is pointed halfway between the center of the drum and the shell, from a distance of six inches. At first, this drum has no EQ. First I'll cut at 300 Hz, next I'll boost the low end at about 80 Hz, then I'll boost the attack at about 4 kHz.

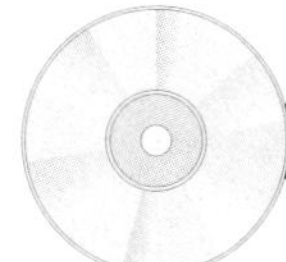

Audio Example 14

Cut 300 Hz, Boost 80 Hz and 4 kHz

Choose your equalization changes with the big picture in mind. If your drum tracks have a lot of isolated tom fills which need to sound full and powerful, leave some low frequency power in the track. It might be necessary to change EQ throughout the course of the track. Don't boost the same high frequencies on each track. The overheads might respond well to a boost of all frequencies above 7–10 kHz. Conversely, a tom track might sound best with a narrow bandwidth boosted at 4 kHz, or so.

Kick Drum

The kick drum (bass drum) is very important to the impact of the drum sound.

Different styles demand different kick sounds. Some sounds, like jazz and heavy rock kicks, have less dampening and ring longer.

Typical Kick Drum EQ

The actual amount of cut or boost you use is solely dependent on what it takes to get the sound you want out of the instrument you're miking. First use mic choice and placement to get the best and most musical sound, then use the amount of EQ necessary to create the appropriate sound.

A low-frequency boost between 75 and 150 Hz adds a low, powerful thump to the kick drum sound.

A mid-frequency cut between 250 and 500 Hz helps clean up the thick, cloudy sound of a close-miked kick.

A high frequency boost between 3 and 5 kHz adds definition, attack and impact to the kick drum sound.

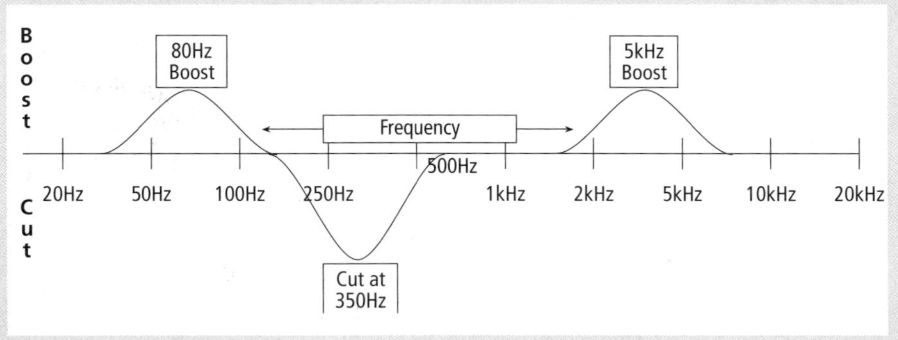

Often in the jazz idiom and some hard rock settings, the kick is not dampened, but the most common kick sound is lightly muffled, with good low-end thump and a clean attack. To achieve this sound, remove the front head and place a blanket or a pillow in the bottom of the drum. The blanket or pillow should be positioned for the desired amount of dampening—the more contact with the head, the more muffling. The weight of the pillow or blanket affects the sound. I've found that a down pillow works great; I'll usually place a brick or a mic stand base on the pillow to hold it in place.

For a little more tone, leave the front head on the drum, still dampening inside using a pillow or blanket. It has become popular to cut a 6–8 inch hole in the front head, typically slightly off-center. Use this hole to position the mic inside or slightly outside the drum. Move the mic in or out to achieve the balance of tone and attack that best supports your music.

A moving-coil mic, positioned inside the kick about six inches from the drummer's head and about halfway between the center of the head and the shell, will usually produce a good sound.

Experiment with mic placement to get the best sound you can before you equalize the sound. On any drum, the attack is strongest at the center of the drum, and the tone is strongest toward the shell. Move the mic to the center of the head if you want more attack. If you need more tone, move the mic toward the shell.

Audio Example 15 demonstrates the sound of a kick drum with the mic inside the drum pointing directly at the center of the head where the beater hits, from a distance of six inches. Notice the attack.

Audio Example 15

Kick Attack

Audio Example 16 demonstrates the same kick as Audio Example 15 with the same mic aimed at the head about two inches in from the shell and about six inches from the head. Notice the tone.

Audio Example 16

Kick Tone

Another factor in the sound of the kick is the distance of the mic from the drum head. Audio Example 17 demonstrates the kick with the mic three inches from the head and about halfway between the center of the head and the drum shell.

Audio Example 17

Kick Three Inches Away

The mic in Audio Example 18 is about one foot outside of the drum, still pointed about half way between the center and the shell.

Kick 12 Inches Outside

As you can tell by these different examples, positioning is critical to the sound of the drum. Not only is the placement of the mic critical, but the tuning of the drum can make all the difference. The tension should be even around the head and there should be appropriate dampening for the sound you need. It's common to hear a very deep sounding kick that has a solid thump in the low end and a good attack. In search of this kind of sound, most drummers tend to loosen the head to get a low sound. This can be a mistake. If the head is tuned too low, the pitch of the drum can be unusable and might not even be audible. To get a warm, punchy thump out of a kick, try tightening the head.

Another very important consideration in the kick sound is the drummer's technique. Drummers that stab at the kick with the beater can choke an otherwise great sound into an unappealing stutter-slap.

Snare Drum

Snare drums usually fall into one of two categories: very easy to get a good sound out of or almost impossible to get good sounds out of. Fortunately there are some tricks we can pull out of the hat to help the more difficult drums sound good. It's important for you to know some quick and easy techniques for getting the snare to work. It's amazing how many decent drummers are lost when it comes to drum sounds.

First, make sure the heads are in good shape. A lot of times the top snare head has been stretched and dented so much that the center of the head is actually loose and sagging, even though the rest of the head is tight. This isn't good. Replacing the head will make a huge difference in the sound.

The heads need to be in good shape. If you're doing much drum recording, it's best to have some extra heads on hand.

A good snare sound is dependent on a lot of factors working perfectly together. If you can handle drum-tuning basics, it'll make a big difference in the sound of your live drum recordings, plus you'll have an insight and perspective on drums that'll prove to be a valuable asset.

Toms

Recording toms is similar in many ways to recording the kick drum and snare drum. It's important that the heads are in good shape, that they're tuned properly and that the dampening gets the appropriate sound for the track. Tune the top and bottom heads to the same tone and be sure the tension is even around each head.

If you want more attack in the sound, move the mic toward the center of the drum, but keep it out of the drummer's way. A miked drum sound has more attack when the microphone is positioned near the center of the drum and more tone when the microphone is positioned near the rim.

Choose reverb for the toms that blends with the snare sound. It's normal to use the same reverb on the toms that you use on the snare. If you use another reverb sound, be sure it complements the overall sound of the snare drum. Avoid selecting sounds that indicate completely different acoustical environments unless you're intentionally conforming to a musical judgment.

Listen to the different tom sounds in Audio Example 19. Note what you like and dislike about each sound. Is the sound boomy? How do the lows sound? Can you hear the attack? Does the drum sound full? Is the drum thin sounding? Do you hear much tone?

Audio Example 19

Lots of Toms

Overhead Microphones

Once you've positioned the close microphones for the snare, kick and toms, use mics over the drums to capture the cymbals and fill in the overall sound of the drums. It's amazing how much separation we can achieve close-miking the kit. One or two mics over the drums are essential to a blended, natural sound.

Position condenser microphones in a stereo pattern (like the examples of a two-mic setup). A good pattern to use is the standard X-Y configuration, with the microphones pointing down at the set at a 90 degree angle to each other. This will provide the excellent stereo image necessary for a big drum sound and will work well in mono.

If the drummer's kit is large and covers a wide area try spreading the X-Y out. Move the microphones away from each other, but be sure they're still pointing away from each other. Also, keep the microphones on the same horizontal plane to minimize adverse phase interactions when listening to the mix in mono.

Overheads on a close-miked kit give definition and position to the cymbals and fill in the overall sound. There isn't much need for the low frequencies since the close microphones give each drum a full, punchy sound. I'll usually roll the lows off below about 150 Hz, and I'll often boost a high frequency between 10 and 15 kHz, to give extra shimmer to the cymbals.

We want the overheads to accurately capture the transient information. Since the transient level exceeds the average level by as much as 9 dB, recording levels on the overheads should read between -7 and -9VU at the peaks to ensure accurately recorded transients. Digital meters should not reach overload (OL).

Wide Stereo Overheads

For a wide stereo image, use two cardioid condenser microphones over the drum set spaced 1–3 inches apart. The mics should be at 90 degree angles to each other and pointing away from each other. If you point the mics toward each other, you'll encounter problems, especially when summing the stereo mix to mono.

Pan the overheads hard right and hard left for the most natural sound. The X-Y technique will provide a sound that is evenly spread across the stereo spectrum. The overheads in Audio Example 20 are about three feet above the cymbals in an

X-Y configuration and are panned hard right and hard left. The lows below 150 Hz are rolled off, and the highs are boosted at 12 kHz.

Audio Example 20

X-Y Panned Hard

We can add different character to the sound of the drums by moving the overheads closer to or farther from the kit. Positioning the mic farther away from the set includes more room sound on the track. This can be good or bad depending on the acoustics of the recording environment.

It isn't typically necessary to add reverb to the overheads in a close-miked configuration. The reverb on the snare and toms is usually sufficient to get a smooth, blended sound.

The Hi-hat Mic

Sometimes it's desirable to put a separate mic on the hi-hat. The choice for or against a hi-hat mic should be based on the style of music and the importance of the hi-hat in the drum part. Most of the time the microphones on the kick, snare, toms and overheads pick up plenty of hi-hat, but a separate track for the hat adds definition to the hi-hat attack and provides pan control in the mix.

Audio Example 21

Panning the Hi-hat

Hi-hats Miked at the Edge

1. Miking the hi-hats at the edge of the cymbals produces a thick, gong-like sound that's not usable for most recording situations.

2. In this position, the air coming from the cymbals closing can cause a loud popping sound as it hits the mic diaphragm.

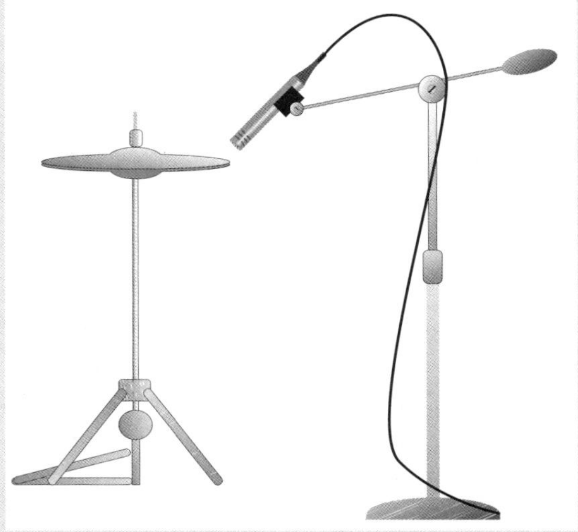

Audio Example 22 demonstrates the sound of a hi-hat miked at the outer edge.

Audio Example 22

Hi-hat Miked at the Outer Edge

Miking the Bell of the Hi-hat

1. Miking the hi-hats at the bell of the top cymbal produces a good, clean sound with plenty of highs. The sound at the bell of the cymbal contains very little of the gong-like sound that comes from miking the edge of the cymbal.

2. The microphone must be at least 3 inches from the cymbal to minimize the change in phase interaction between the cymbal and the mic capsule (caused by opening and closing the hi-hat).

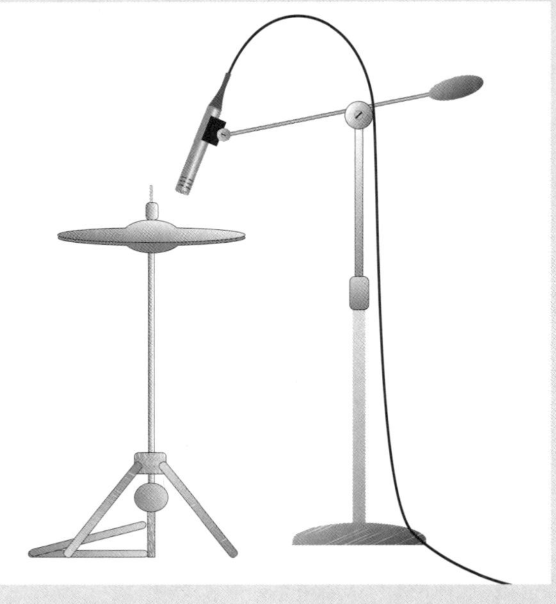

Audio Example 23 demonstrates the sound of the hi-hat with the mic pointing down at the bell of the top cymbal.

Audio Example 23

Hi-hat Miked at the Bell

Gating the Drum Tracks

Sometimes we need to isolate the drum tracks, either to equalize them separately, to pan them or to add effects to an individual instrument or group of instruments.

Patch the drum track through a gate. Adjust the attack time to its fastest setting and the release time to about half a second. Adjust the range control so that everything below the threshold will be turned off. Finally, adjust the threshold so that the gate only opens when the drum is hit. This will isolate the drum. Once the drum is isolated, you can process it alone with minimal effect on the rest of the kit. For example, you can add as much reverberation as you want without leakage adding reverb to the rest of the drums. Listen to the kit in Audio Example 24. I'll solo the snare track, then adjust the gate to get rid of the leakage between the snare hits.

Audio Example 24

Adjusting The Gate

Once the gate is adjusted properly, you can put drastic amounts of reverb on the snare by itself. Listen to Audio Example 25 as I put a lot of reverb on this gated snare track.

Audio Example 25

Reverb on the Gated Snare

In Audio Example 26, listen to the complete kit with a lot of reverb on the gated snare track. After a few seconds, I'll bypass the gate on the snare. Notice the change in the reverb.

Audio Example 26

Bypassing the Gate

Application of Techniques

Aiming the Mics

It's important to get into the habit of aiming microphones away from sounds you want to exclude from a track. Use the cardioid pickup patterns to your advantage. For example, if you're miking a hi-hat and the mic is pointed at the bell of the top cymbal, that's good. Not only should you point the mic at the bell of the hi-hat, but you should point the back of the mic at a cymbal that's close by. Pointing the back of the hi-hat mic at the crash cymbal helps minimize the amount of crash that is recorded by the hi-hat mic. Use the cardioid pickup pattern to reject the unwanted sound while it captures the intended sound.

Minimizing Leakage

1. Aim the cardioid mic at the bell of the hi-hat to pick up a good, clean hi-hat sound.

2. Position the microphone so that it aims directly away from the instrument you want to minimize—in this case it's the crash cymbal. This technique won't eliminate an unwanted instrument, but it will decrease leakage and increase separation.

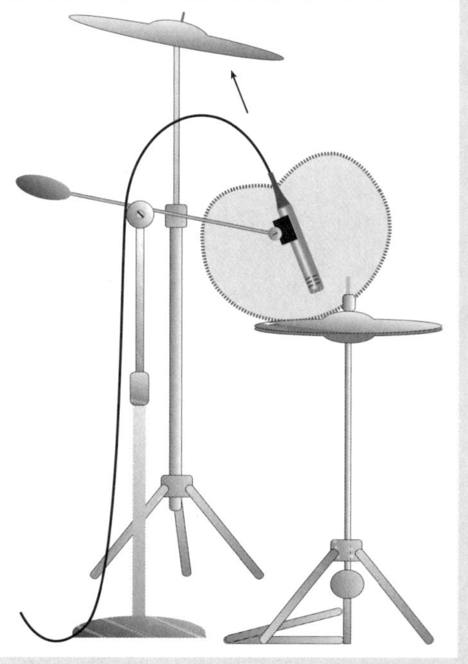

Phones

It's necessary for the drummer to have a good, well-balanced headphone mix. Headphones are the best way for the drummer to monitor the rest of the musicians or tracks. A good drummer is always trying to lock in to a strong rhythmic feel with the rest of the group. The drummer and bass player, especially, need to hear each other well. Be sure both the bass player and the drummer can hear the attack of the kick, snare and hi-hat. Don't make them guess where the beat is. Adjusting the headphone mix can be your most important contribution to the feel of a song. Listen to the headphone mix yourself through headphones, so that you can tell exactly what the players are hearing. Respond to their requests for changes in level. Spending the time to make the phones an asset rather than a detriment is time well spent.

Baffles, Gobos, Screens

Ideally, the drums will be the only sound in the room at the time they're being recorded. This provides ultimate flexibility during mixdown. However, there are times when guitar, bass and drums must be recorded in the same room, usually due to a lack of space or time. When this happens, isolate the instruments as much as you can. Use baffles around the drums to shield the drum microphones from other sounds. Baffles are small, freestanding partitions with either two soft, absorptive sides or one soft side and one hard reflective side. They typically measure about four feet square and are four to eight inches thick. They're also called gobos or screens.

When baffling drums be aware of the surfaces behind the drum set. Hard reflective surfaces behind the kit send strong reflections all around any room. Baffles are often as effective behind the drums as they are in front.

Baffles can also be placed around the guitar amp, or blankets can be placed over the amp and the mic. The blanket will shield the guitar mic from unwanted sounds, plus it'll muffle the guitar to help keep it from the drum mics or other microphones in the room.

Gobos, Baffles, and Screens

Place baffles around the drums to isolate the mics from other live instruments in the studio. A baffle will only effectively isolate frequencies smaller than it is. The overheads in this illustration are obviously not baffled; additionally, neither are the low frequencies longer than four feet.

There is still value in using this baffle setup. The baffles do more than just minimize leakage into the drum mics; they also decrease the drum set volume in the room, therfore minimizing leakage of the drums into other instrument or vocal mics.

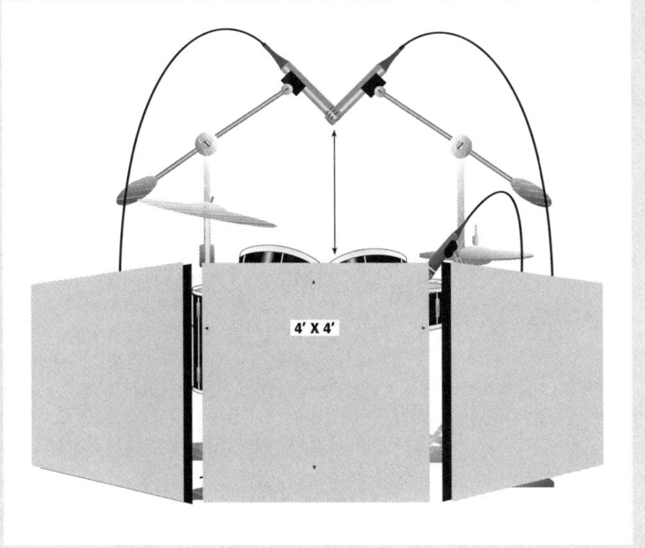

Though we strive for ultimate separation between tracks and complete control over the sound of each instrument, some great recordings have been achieved with the entire band in one room playing the tracks live. Blues, jazz, some country and some rock styles can benefit from the natural, open sound that a live, one-room recording offers.

Click Track

One feature of a professional sounding recording is a solid rhythmic feel that maintains an even and constant tempo. A sure sign of an amateur band and an amateur recording is a loose rhythmic feel that radically speeds up and slows down.

Most drummers need some assistance to maintain a constant tempo. We call this assistance the click track. A click track can simply be a steady metronome pulse, like that from a drum machine or an electronic metronome. It gives the drummer a rhythmic reference to keep the tempo steady.

A drum machine is a good source for the click because it offers the ability to change the sound. Click sounds with good transients work the best because the transient attack unquestionably defines the placement of the beat.

It's very important that the drummer hears the click well, but the biggest problem with a click track is leakage of the sound of the click from the headphones into the drum microphones. It's difficult to deal with click leakage into the overheads on a quiet or texturally open part of a song. The click has to be at a certain level for the drummer to hear it, but if it's too loud and is audible on the drum microphones, the drum track might not be usable. The solution lies in finding headphones that enclose the drummer's ears well enough to conceal click from the microphones. There are many phones available that will perform well. They usually have solid housings and fluid or air-filled soft plastic pads that completely surround the ears.

Effects On Drums

Whenever possible wait until mixdown to add reverb if you have enough tracks to print each drum to its own track. You won't really know the impact of the effects on the entire mix until the mix is up and running.

If you're combining the drums to one or two tracks at the time of the initial recording but have a separate mic for each drum, you might need to print the reverb to the multitrack. This will be the only time in the recording process where you'll have individual to reverb sends. This process can work well, but it takes practice and experience to second-guess what the track will really sound like in the final mix.

The amount of reverb and ambience that you incorporate in your drum sounds depends on stylistic and musical factors. We seem to seesaw from very wet sounds to very dry sounds in all pop genres. It's up to you to stay in tune with the trends in your musical arena. Be informed to create a competitive and commercial sound, or at least know what you're doing when you break all the rules in pop-dom.

Remember, the more reverb you apply to any sound, the further away and less intimate it feels.

Compressing Drums

Compression is a common drum recording and mixing technique. Compression has two primary effects on drum tracks. First, since the compressor is an automatic level control, it evens out the volume of each hit. This can be a very good thing on a commercial rock tune. The compressor keeps the level even so that a weak hit doesn't detract from the groove.

The second benefit of compression is its ability, with proper use, to accentuate the attack of the drum. If the compressor controls are adjusted correctly, we can exaggerate the attack of the drum, giving it a very aggressive and penetrating edge. This technique involves setting the attack time of the compressor slow enough so that the attack isn't compressed but the remaining portion of the sound is.

This is how to set the compressor to exaggerate the attack of any drum:

1. Set the ratio between 3:1 and 10:1.
2. Set the release time at about .5 seconds. This will need to be adjusted according to the length of the snare sound. Just be sure the LEDs showing gain reduction have all gone off before the next major hit of the drum. This doesn't apply to fills, but if the snare is hitting on 2 and 4, the LEDs should be out before each hit.
3. At this point, set the attack time to its fastest setting.
4. Adjust the threshold for 3 to 9 dB of gain reduction.

5. Finally, readjust the attack time. As you slow the attack time of the compressor, it doesn't react in time to compress the transient, but it can react in time to compress the rest of the drum sound.

Exaggerating the Snare Transient

This graph shows the sound energy of a snare drum without compression. (Threshold and attack time are only indicated as references.) The threshold is set above the attack of the drum so there is no compression occurring.

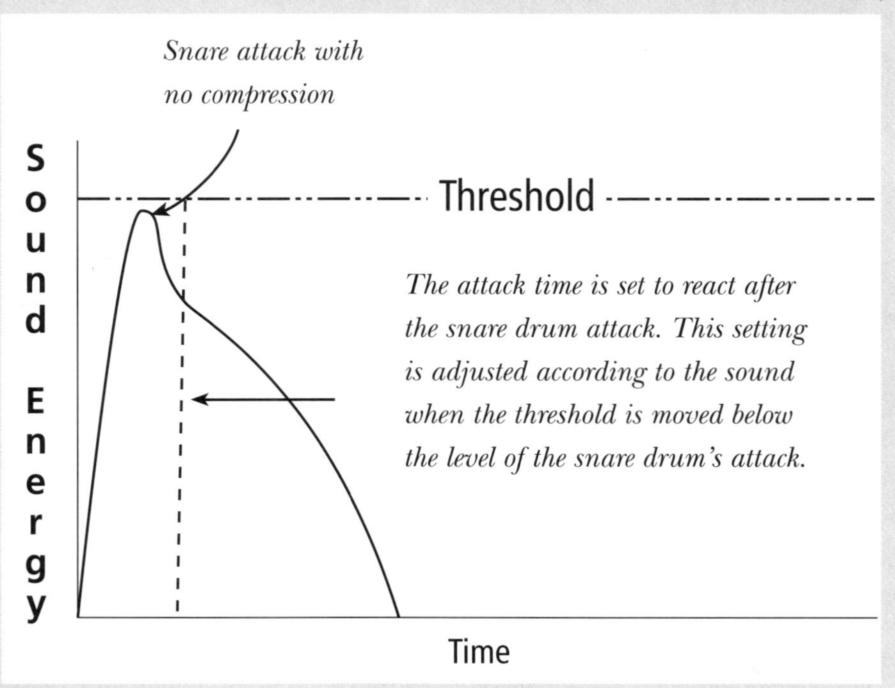

The Result of Compression

Exaggerated attack is the result of compressing the snare after the attack. When set like this, the attack isn't turned down by the VCA but the body of the snare sound is.

Notice the attack time is set to react after the attack of the snare drum. This setting is made by ear. Adjust the attack time until you hear the exaggerated attack.

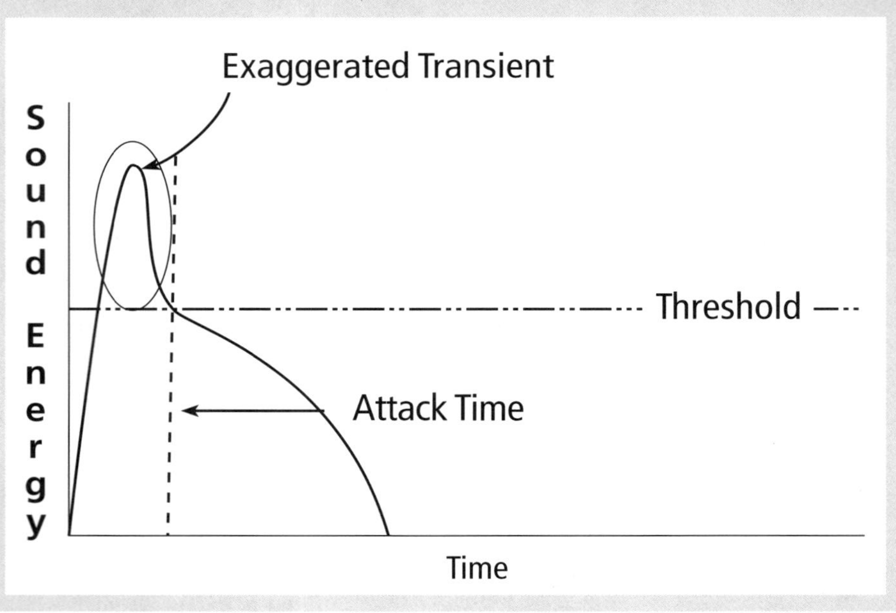

Panning the Drums

Panning the drum requires a decision about the concept of the final mix. If you're trying to create a final product that sounds like a live band with a live drummer, you'll need to pan accordingly. Imagine the drummer's position on stage, and place all of the drums within that space. Since the drums are usually center stage, the toms are usually panned very close around the center when using this approach.

Panning from high to low between about 10 and 2 o'clock can still give the impression of the drums being center stage while clearing out the middle of the stereo image for lead instruments.

Kick and snare drums are almost always panned center since they provide the foundation of the mix. The low-frequency content of the kick needs to be dispersed evenly between the left-right spectrum and the constant repetition of the snare dictates it's center position. A snare, panned to one side or the other continually pulls the listener to that side and distracts from the balanced feel of a mix.

Overheads are often panned hard left and right. The acoustic mix of the drums in the room keeps them grouped together in most settings.

Toms, panned hard left to hard right can interrupt the natural feel of a mix.

Listen to the drum balance through a good set of headphones. Some pan settings sound good on monitor speakers but are very distracting in headphones. If you ignore these guidelines, do it intentionally with great artistic and musically resolve.

Compare Your Work

I've never known anyone that didn't want their work to sound competitive next to other commercially released music. Check your work against your favorite album in your genre. Set up the mixer so the reference CD is playing at the same time as your mix. Select back and forth between the two, evaluating how they compare sonically. This is very instructional. Listen specifically to the high, mid, and low-frequency content.

The most difficult frequencies to dial in are the lows. It's important to be very selective and intentional when boosting and cutting low frequencies. When the same low frequency is boosted on several instruments (kick, bass, guitar, keys, etc.) energy accumulates and the mix level becomes artificially hot—the meters register hot but the mix sounds cold.

To create a mix that's powerful and punchy, start with the drum and bass mix. Where you boost low frequencies on one instrument cut low frequencies on another. Fit the mix together like a jigsaw puzzle throughout the frequency spectrum.

It's more important to establish a clean attack on each drum track than it is to establish powerful lows. When you turn down the midrange, you'll find that both the lows and highs can be heard better.

Continue to craft your mix until it matches the reference CD in every way.

At The Same Meter Reading Does It Sound As Loud?

- If not, try fitting your equalizations together tighter.
- On a track that doesn't need lows, roll them off to the point where you can just start to hear a difference (high-pass filters work best for this).

- On a track that doesn't need highs, roll them off to the point where you can just start to hear a difference (low-pass filters work best for this).
- Try eliminating some ingredients from the mix. Simpler is louder.
- Locate ingredients that might be momentarily causing deceptively high levels. Toms are often the guilty party where this is concerned. If the low frequencies are turn up too far on a floor tom, your mix might go crazy every time the drum is hit. Typically, the mixing engineer can't even hear the frequencies that are causing the buildup. Turning the low frequencies down on the floor tom often provides the perfect cure—the drum still sounds just as good and the mix level is controlled.

Does Your Mix Sound As Clean In The High Frequencies As The Reference?

- It's amazing how bright many commercial pop mixes are. This is true because experienced mix engineers have discovered that a bright mix cuts through on the radio. They've also discovered that if a mix is a little devoid of low frequencies the problem is easily repaired during mastering. In addition, they've gotten the maximum level on the master media, providing a cleaner, smoother and punchier mix in both the analog and digital realms.

Evaluate the sound of each drum and each instrument for frequency content, comparative level and balance, and musical effect. Once you've completed this process, you'll be amazed at how great your mix is sounding. It is very satisfying to listen to your work and be able to realistically proclaim its competitive integrity.

Triggering During Mixdown

It's common in certain genres to use the recorded drum tracks to trigger sampled drum sounds. I've used this technique and gotten some incredible results. Current digital workstation software facilitates automatic replacement with great ease. Your digitally recorded drum sounds can be replaced with those of your favorite drummers. The libraries of samples are readily available—and they sound really good.

However, this technique can create a sterile and nonmusical mix. It is very difficult to recreate the expression of a real performance on a great kit. Don't let triggered sounds become a copout—a substitution for spending the time to record innovative, fresh, and musical drum sounds. If you use triggered sounds, use them for musical augmentation or if there's just no other way to get decent sounding drum tracks.

There are numerous means to replace recorded sounds with pre-sampled sounds. Verify the approach by consulting the documentation for your software or DAW.

Automation

Take advantage of the automation features available on many of the current mixers, digital software packages, and digital audio workstations. Listen through your song and turn the tom tracks on only when the toms are hit. This will tighten the entire drum sound. Use automated mutes to add precision to releases and punches. Listen carefully to the entire drum part and meticulously craft the drum levels, pans, and EQ.

Then combine the drums and bass. Be sure they're blended and tight. Ride their levels throughout the mix to maintain punch, power, and transparency. I like to add the lead vocal next and automate their levels throughout. Once this is accomplished, the rest of the ingredients have a place to go; you know where they're need and where they're not needed.

Conclusion

All of the techniques and principals contained in this book work during tracking and in final mixdown. Build the drums from the kick drum to the overheads. Strive to maintain intimacy while, at the same time, providing the illusion of controlled size and depth. Have fun developing your drum sound.